Don't Take My
Word for It...
See for Yourself

# Don't Take My Word for It... See for Yourself

Taneka Lewis

Cover art by Loren Jaxson

To the ones that have been through some unexpected

shit:


You are not alone.

Give yourself grace, not only because you need it — but

because you deserve it!

Uncertain if her affection was for him or for the version of herself that she became in his presence.

How can you differentiate between genuine affection towards a person or if you like who you are when you're with them?

He led her to where he wanted her to go then turned to

ask her how they got here...

Have you ever been led somewhere you didn't ask to go?

The shallowness of our relationship was exposed when I no longer needed you for validation.

What has exposed the shallowness of your relationships?

She sat in what felt like constant grief,

while he crumbled beneath the weight of her

expectations.

Describe the grief you have experienced from trying to

uphold a false image of yourself to please someone else.

She'd dig deeper to get closer to him,

hoping he'd become the mask she gave to him,

to meet the expectations she never communicated,

and give her what he actually didn't possess.

She'd keep digging until there was nothing left,

until she came up empty and angry that she never gave

who he presented a real chance.


Whose image did you fight so hard to get close to that

you never gave the real them a chance?

He thought a bottle could take him away from where he was, to a place where he believed he yearned for. Yet, it only carried him further from where he needed to be. A deceptive illusion.

When did you realize that trying to run away from your "problems" only brought you right back to what you need to deal with?

You tried to edit me like your My Player on 2k,

instead of accepting me for who I was.

That wasn't love.

When did you notice they tried to change you?

You took everything you wanted, while I thought I gave

you what you needed.

In the end I came out empty, wasting time not being me.

Was everything you wanted what you needed?

She diminished her abilities which gave him the power to devalue what she offered.

How many times have you suppressed your abilities by giving power to the wrong one?

He won't give you the respect you don't show yourself.

How can you show yourself the respect you deserve from others?

Her love thrived on communicating the truth, while his ego fed off the perception of the truth he created.

What is the foundation of your love? What does your love feed on? Can you see love through your disagreements?

She set boundaries because she didn't trust him with the intimate parts of her anymore.

What boundaries have you set to protect yourself?

His actions revealed his inconsistencies, so she gave him unavailability.

How do you reward inconsistency?

She longed for his touch beyond pleasure, in places his
hands couldn't reach.

She craved to be in the presence of his energy, for the
interaction of the connection of their souls, and
to be a part of the depths of their conversations.

Thirsting for the experiences of intangible intimacy.

Is (s)he someone you can experience intangible intimacy
with?

He wanted to be held, but not be soothed.

She wanted to cuddle, but not be touched.

He wanted a connection without communication.

She wanted intimacy, but not to be vulnerable.

He wanted safety but wouldn't dare fall apart to be seen.

They wanted what they were incapable of doing for

themselves.

What do you want from someone else that you're not

willing to do for yourself?

She fed herself false narratives based on how she thought he wanted her to show up. Eventually, she realized he didn't deserve how she showed up for him if she couldn't be her true self.

Is your true self different from how they want you to show up?

His obsession and commitment to protecting her heart inadvertently led him to hurt her with lack of transparency and honesty.

When have your intentions caused pain that you didn't plan to do?

I lost myself when I trusted your hands to nurture me,

your heart to pour life into me, your soul to feed me.

Whose hands have you lost yourself in?

I wanted to give you access, but the key I gave you didn't open the door that I was behind.

How often do we give people keys to doors we aren't behind?

She felt stuck between protecting herself from repeating past experiences and giving him a chance because he wasn't the one responsible for her scars.

Who haven't you given a fair chance because of scars given to you by someone else?

I fought against being wrong because I'd have to forgive

myself, but it's my destiny to be set free -

Free from this;

Free from you.

What's worse, being wrong or being forgiven?

She empathized with him, but his healing wasn't her responsibility no matter how much she cared about and loved him.

How much responsibility have you given yourself for someone else's healing?

You didn't consider the trauma, pain, or hurt he carried

as you selfishly threw expectations at him,

not knowing if he could even attempt to meet them.

What expectations have you thrown at someone not

knowing if they could even meet them?

He's lost, hating her for knowing what direction she's going.

He wants what his friends have without knowing what they went through to get it.

He's holding onto fairytales not knowing if it's worth the space it's taking up.

Will he let go?

You want the idea of what someone has, but are you willing to go through what it took for them to get it?

He told his story in spaces that were created for you to just listen. You projected your unwarranted perspective during the amplification of his vulnerability.
And slowly his reluctance met the presence of your inconsideration.

Do you cultivate spaces for people to vent and be heard or just space for you to feel like you helped fix their "problem"?

I overanalyzed every detail of our interaction.

Is it me ... is it him ... or is it us?

Frustrated that I wouldn't let myself be;

Be who I naturally wanted;

Be who I authentically am;

Out of fear of getting what I actually want,

what I actually need

I never gave myself, you, or us ... a full chance.


When have you sabotaged what you wanted?

I'm not responsible for meeting the expectations of the labels you place on me.

What labels have other people placed on you? What expectations have come with them?

Incomplete without intimacy;

incapable of feeling what I think I miss when I look at

you.

How does the lack of intimacy affect your relationships?

Holding the pieces of her heart

that reflected her broken trust,

she laid in shattered glass without belief in his ability to

carefully handle her vulnerability.

Who don't you trust with your vulnerability?

She needed herself more than she wanted him to need her.

How do you show up for yourself when you need you?

She thought she knew what love was until she had to forgive you.

How has the power of forgiveness redefined how you define love?

Her love grew as she nurtured her inner child; providing herself the love she needed while growing up gave her the opportunity to address the insecurities of her childhood.

What does your inner child need at the height of your emotions?

He knew how to love her because she loved herself in the ways she wanted to receive love before they met.

How do you show love to yourself?

The value of our relationship wasn't tainted by the quantity of our communication.

Is the value of your relationship defined by how much you talk or the depth and quality of what you talk about?

She was never enough until she met him.

When did you feel you were enough for him?

He communicated to articulate his true feelings, not to echo what he believed she desired to hear.

How can you enhance your communication to ensure you effectively articulate your true feelings?

Love. The thing we think we'll never find, but the thing we run fastest away from when it comes.

How is it that the thing you desire most is the thing you're most afraid of?

Disengaging from her emotions only brought her closer

to the truth of what she felt.

What truth has your emotions shown you?

Taneka Lewis

She let external influences dictate how she showed up based on the ideals they placed on her.

How have the ideals of others affected how you show up?

She doubted what she defined for herself because she thought their validation meant more.

Whose validation holds weight when defining yourself?

Taneka Lewis

In the midst of processing other people's actions,

She felt consumed by things she had no say in,

Wondering where,

Wondering how she fit into it all.

How often do you let other people's actions consume

you?

She grew tired of not feeling like enough

to people she held in positions

that she expected to empower her.

When will you be enough for yourself?

She doubted herself and felt she was inadequate. She wasn't enough and she would never be enough until she accepted herself for who she was, with or without you here.

What does your journey of self-acceptance and acknowledging your worth look like?

Compassion forced her to look at her hurt from your perspective. It shined a light on the darkness where she labeled your pain. It gave her clarity on the things that her wounds blinded.

How have labels clouded the clarity of your wounds?

I knew you could provide for me, but I yearned for you to teach me the essence of love – what it is, what feels like, what looks like, what it should be so that as I grew up, I wouldn't search for it in places it would never be.

Where did you find love? Did you find it in the place(s) you thought it would be?

I evened the playing field to feel and touch your

vulnerability and watch it interact with mine,

humanizing the people I held in high places to put their

flaws into perspective.

When was the first time you realized the people you hold

to a higher precedence are human too?

There is no love lost

I respect and thank you,

but you are no longer in the position you once were,

so, I no longer hold you to meet the expectations I once

had.

Who is someone you no longer hold to meet the

expectations you once had for them?

She couldn't beat him up

for not knowing what she needed

or being equipped to provide it,

but she felt sorry he wasn't able to love her like she felt

she needed to be loved.

When did you realize they weren't capable of giving you

what you needed or what you thought you needed?

He's a good person, but that did not dictate whether he was a good influence for where she wanted her life to go. That didn't make him a bad person either, but she had to check her inventory.

When have you felt bad for having to let go of a good person that no longer fit into the direction your life was going?

Her true growth lies in the power of understanding how her trauma affects her daily decisions, not just acknowledging that it happened.

How do triggers and trauma affect your daily decisions?

Trying to live life with her head on a swivel to not
misstep,

she tripped where her boundaries were,

readjusting them to sustain her evolution.

How has your evolution adjusted your boundaries?

Unpacking stacked trauma and disassembling the source

of triggers;

I needed gentleness and grace with myself the most to

grant myself the freedom to learn and adapt to new

discoveries about my past.

Exploring new paths on my healing journey I found that

things are different here.

How has grace and gentleness with yourself impacted

your healing?

Her reflection told her what she didn't have the courage to tell herself.

When was the last time you looked in the mirror?

I developed the habit of labeling emotions before

embracing their experience; neglecting the opportunity

to feel,

to listen,

to understand, and

to truly observe;

their presence is a guide to explore myself deeper.

When have you taken the time to fully experience your

emotions?

She beats herself up for past mistakes, holding onto

things that are familiar and certain,

but are no longer in her walk of truth.

She projects them into her future

all while desperately hoping for a different outcome.

Stepping out of insanity won't work while holding the

weight of things that once were.

What are you still holding on to that is keeping you

trapped in insanity?

She hoarded her gifts because

she'd been hurt before using the platform she was blessed

with, keeping them to herself sharing only pieces to

protect her from exposing her insecurities.

She didn't realize her security lied in the act of releasing.

Releasing the trauma that couldn't go where she was

headed.

What gifts are you hoarding that's keeping you from fully

living out your purpose?

I watched her go through heartbreak again.

She deserved better, yet she stayed.

Sometimes lessons have to come before we can see the

truth.


What lessons have you learned before you saw your

truth?

Everything comes with a price.

Are you willing to tolerate the bad that comes with the good?

Can you eliminate the distractions?

Are you equipped to stay focused on your path?

Can you meet the demands of discipline?

Is the freedom to define yourself worth the sacrifice?

What price are you willing to pay?

What are you worth?

Her energy attracted the people she needed to expose the cracks in her foundation she didn't want to face.

They held her accountable to fill the space with more of herself and less of him, them.

Who do you have to hold you accountable? Does your energy attract people that are going to hold you accountable?

Imposter syndrome an imposter in itself...

green grass will always be green when it's fake.

Open your eyes and look at the grass beneath your feet; it

goes through seasons too.

There are weeds, there are brown patches...

but when properly watered it always grows back in the

season it's supposed to arise.

How are you nurturing the things necessary for your

growth in this current season?

Her confidence shined bright when she had you in her hand.

She was in control and nothing seemed to penetrate her armor,

but everything shifted when she let you go.

Every rejection seemed to pierce through,

leaving space for doubt and insecurity tempting to rush her into isolation

where she could overthink and  overanalyze her problems.

As the silence choked her, it whispered,

"You possess no problem to which you can't find a solution."


When have you doubted your ability to find or be a solution to a problem?

Fear of repeating generational patterns fueled her actions with hesitation and contentment.

She was stuck between losing the motivation to live out what she desired and accepting what felt like her unfortunate reality.

Would she ever find love?

How do generational patterns influence your actions?

I held it in for as long as I could.

I knew when I took a deep breath, I'd feel the weight of
your absence.

My heart felt heavy as cement and delicate as glass.

It ached knowing I couldn't talk to you or hear your
laugh.

But when I felt a tingle of warmth, I knew your spirit
came to wrap me in your arms with a big smile.

Whose spirit gives you warmth when they're no longer
physically here?

I sat back as I watched the stream of thoughts pop up.

I didn't cling to them and spiral down an emotional
tornado.

I removed myself and let my thoughts exist as an entity
outside of me;

I was intrigued to discover the root of my scattered
thoughts.

Proud of the access I'd given myself to reach depths only
detachment could provide, I experienced the power &
bliss of self.

What practices can you implement to explore greater
depths of yourself?

She grew frustrated with feeling like she needed to be corrected to be understood.

Do your emotions have the freedom to be understood without correction?

She looked in the mirror wanting to see what you saw,

the things you missed and overlooked when you looked

at her.

You shaped what the mirror reflected back into her

mind, her heart and what she carried out into the world.

Your words erased parts of her before she had the chance

to see them, before she had the chance to show you the

vastness of her value, tending to tainted territory.

Who has shaped how you look at yourself; how you look

at your value?

Taneka Lewis

We sit in our trauma because we're afraid of the discomfort that comes with gaining from a loss.

What discomfort are you willing to face to see gains from a loss?

Losses disqualify what no longer serves us.

What have you lost that no longer serves you?

I thought because I identified and accepted my past it would no longer affect my future, yet it crept in until forgiveness shut the door and locked it behind me. I had space to make room for my new growth.

What keeps creeping back into your life that needs to be forgiven?

Confidence through the roof and fully capable yet

wondering where she went wrong and if she was actually

enough...

The confidence of self-doubt.

When have you felt like you weren't enough?

She forgave herself.

She did what she thought she had to do.

It's not her fault, but it's her responsibility to release it

for healing.

What do you need to release for your healing?

Her insecurities and fears had her running from what was good for her, but as clarity and confidence came, her patterns shifted.

How long have you let insecurities and fear hold you back from shifting your perspective?

She loved herself enough to not stand in her own way of forgiveness.

Do you love yourself enough to get out of your way?

She found comfort in being uncomfortable with herself.

She chose not to be loyal to the old version of herself.

How uncomfortable are you willing to get to experience a new version of yourself?

She loved herself enough to trust her body,

to listen to what it needed,

to embrace what it reflected back to her in the mirror.

Dismissing what magnified her insecurities.

She pushed herself to love her flaws and all.

She was and will always be enough.

Are you enough for you?

I fell in love with risking it all because I had more to lose with not being all in.

Are you afraid of what you might gain if you risk it all?

You're allowed to own you -

Your space;

Your thoughts;

Your perspective;

Your value;

Your worth;

Your dreams;

Your passions;

Your love.

Don't put you in the hands of someone else without holding yourself first.

Have you held yourself before being held in the hands of someone else?

Her smile radiates with happiness,

free from the things that once held her captive.

How do you celebrate your freedom?

She didn't seek criticism to change herself to meet the criteria you thought she should.
She sought for her authenticity to be accepted in the spaces she chose to be.

When did you realize your authenticity wasn't appreciated in the spaces you wanted it to be?

Searching any and everywhere

For validation from people who can never provide it,

But when she finds herself,

She'll recognize and believe in her worth,

Looking nowhere else.

How did you find your self-worth?

Isolation granted me access

to be in the company of myself,

to navigate the enjoyment of my empty moments,

to satisfy the time I needed with me,

to keep myself company.

Can you sit with the comfortable and uncomfortable

parts of yourself by yourself?

## Don't Take My Word for It

Forced into stillness,

light pierced through the holes in my heart.

Some patch work you did, stitching up my wounds.

Dissolving stitches, you healed my heart a piece at a time;

you gave it a chance to hold the full capacity of what

someone is willing and wanting to pour into it.

How has stillness shown you the areas of you that need
healing?

She continued to dip her brush in paint, noticing that within every struggle, she found small successes that contributed to creating the big picture—the masterpiece.

Have you appreciated your small wins lately?

You are the light in the darkness,

even when you feel like it's consuming you.

Lift your head during your darkest hours.

Your light, it's eternal.

What steps can you take to remind yourself that your

light is eternal, even in darkness?

She walked in boldness,

lived by values,

explored with curiosity,

regardless of fear because

living in her truth outweighed what someone else

thought.

How can you cultivate the courage to walk in your

boldness?

I erased the expiration date I put on my evolution

because it's what's best for me.

I'm willing to sit in the discomfort of my change because

I deserve the better part of me.

I refuse to accept what doesn't align to the cycle of my

growth because I define my value & my worth.

When was the last time you did what was best for you?

She thought the pain broke her,

instead the pain moved her.

The pain sparked a translation to discover strength in a

buried area she would have never dug up.

But she can't be broken,

only transformed by the power within her pain.

When has the power of pain allowed you to experience a

translation?

Everything she desired, craved wouldn't last without
healing.

Her vision only considered embracing the positives,
but this transition was equipping her to work through
the negative compliments.

What life transition helped you learn that with positives
you have to accept negatives as well?

She held onto things that no longer served her.

The world tried to show her the unnecessary things that

didn't belong to her.

She accepted, embraced, and thrived in her new found

freedom.

When will you accept letting go of the things that no

longer serve you?

She trusted the forces outside of herself.

Grounding herself in the season that was created for her to bloom, she sat in frustration and discomfort sacrificing temporary satisfaction while her internal shift was taking place.

She relinquished the fight against everything she had once planned, blindly surrendering to obedience.

When did you get tired of fighting against what was meant to be?

When did you submit to the season you were meant to be in?

Her definition of patience was tested when she had to decide how long she was willing to go without getting frustrated about how long it would take.

When your patience is tested what strategies do you implement to help shift your mindset?

She thrives in the light because she's been in the dark.

She basks in complete being because she knows what it feels like to be broken.

She trusts because someone once never trusted her.

She dreams because it was once all she felt like she could do to escape where she was.

How does where you are show appreciation to where you used to be?

Like the ocean...

There will always be ripples and waves, but they don't

always have to crash.

What techniques can you practice to calm you in high

stress and emotional situations?

You don't have it all figured out because you don't have to have it all figured out.

When did you let go of trying to have it all figured out?

She wrote to express herself and let go, without appreciation and acknowledgement of the art, without love, as her pen kept moving and her healing kept flowing.
She fell in love with seeing the ink of her progress.

What have you gained appreciation and love for as you did it more consistently?

What does the story you tell yourself sound like?

Does this story reflect the truth of reality or just what you tell yourself to make yourself feel better?

Silent enough to listen.

Faith enough to trust.

Obedient enough to take action.